to Burr McCloskey —

Keep the Vision of your mind

Beauty / truth are one

Embrace each Word you use to make peace

Rose Virgo

*Be glad that your shoes are plain
For if they are too red.....*

      Old fairy tale

Just A south-side ~~Girl~~

Rose Virgo

Chicago Stories and other poems

First Printing
Just A south-side Girl © 1990-1993 Rose Virgo.
All Rights Reserved

Cover: Original Illustration and adaptation by
James Morlock © All rights reserved
Four Legged Gent

Inside Photo: Mary Beck

Back Cover Photo: Bill Kucera

Some of these poems have been published in Hammers (doublestar press 1991 and 1992) Poetry Magazine # 4 and # 5, Voices Alive and Women's World. They have also been recorded for Poetman Video.

ISBN 09615879-2-X

Hidden Key Press
P.O. Box 513
Hallandale, Fla. 33008

Distributed by P.H. Press
1446 N. Milwaukee, Chicago, Il. 60622

For those who have loved me
For Anne, Maggie, Rosie and Bernie
For those most dear...

Chicago Stories

Blowin' Down 45th Street 8
Revelation At Eleven 10
The Golden Bush..............................12
Burning Down The Baby Factory 14
A Bottle Of Red 16
Secret Heart Of A Flame................17
The Unicorn Connection...............20

Woman Of Wonder

A Woman On The Edge....................25
New Kind Of Baby......................26
The Eyes Of The Dragon.................28
Too Easy...................................29
Red Hot Mama............................31
A Woman In Love 32
Rhinos In The Moonlight................33
Ticket To Ride.............................34

The Miami Series

Nite Not Alone....................38
I Want To Run.................40
Ode To.........................41.
Unbridled 43
The 60's Aint Over Yet 45
Meeting Allen 47
This Is The House 49
Amid Crashing Iron 52

If The Key Fits

Spa Lady 54
Keys Of Coral Reef ....55.
Key West 56
Key West For Sale 57
Hometown Son 58
Paradise 59

Chicago Stories

Blowin' Down 45th Street

I was a south side girl
with a penchant for night moves
with the bod of a twelve year old
still at fifteen

I grew up south side. Daley's south side. Blue collar spit and polish city workers in the land of the Irish Political Giants due straight east of the pens and the slaughter houses of the old stock yards.

There's an empty lot there now, where the building I grew up in stood. Where Mrs. Luscid's Irish Soda bread wafted through every single flat, every Tuesday afternoon.

Years ago these empty lots would be called prairies. They would be grown over with trees and wildflowers. We would gather there, when I was a kid, in the summer time, right around dusk, then we'd start a fire.
The biggest kid would do it. The rest of us would throw in our potatoes. Now that was the most marvelous smell on that south side air that you could ever smell. The last mouthful of that burnt spud was worth it all. Even gettin' a crack, if you didn't get home on time, when you were suppose to.

I was pretty good at devising some cosmic tale. My best line was, " I was just goin' to check out the ol' angel."

The Angel. That was the angel with the long, long trumpet protected by the high, high iron fence, thoroughly exposed under the street light. She was always under siege.

> " Well...is it still there ? " the crack-giving voice would inquire.

> " Nah, she's been swapped. Musta happened before the street lights went on. "

It was a pretty sure thing that it had happened. Every time the parish would replace that angel Gabriel's horn, some smart ass mick raped it away damn quick. Play Gabriel play. There she stood, solid gold, wavy statued hair billowing behind. Standing there with those out stretched arms...just playing the air.

I went back there a couple of years ago. I drove down 45th street just so I could check her out. There she stood solid gold as ever, never to feel a long horned trumpet pressed against those stone heavenly lips.

Goes to show ya...some things never change.

Revelation At Eleven

Cold hard steel against my cheeks
felt strange
he stared back
at me

His fingers fumbled
as if he were adjusting
some imaginary instrument

no place to play

Food came
he moved slightly
not to reach out for it
but to see his jailer
look him in the eye

He made no effort to eat

no place to feast

He was magnificent
masses of muscle
one swift movement
could damage any opponent
or draw
his lady love close
a family man
if I ever saw one

no place to mate

Others laughed
moved away
his eyes stayed locked to mine
after a time
I started talking
telling him about myself
what I wanted to be
he listened to every word
then
he offered his hand
I reached through
the blue steel barrier
would never reach it
massive and silent
he just kept staring at me
his eyes began to water
a tear brimmed
on the edge

Here sat the hairiest
most talked of
feared
giant of his kind
in captivity

My conversation
with the great Bushman
taught me before I was 12
that I would rather die
than be prisoner
in such a caring
intellectually astute society

At eleven
those were the saddest eyes
I'd ever seen

The Golden Bush

Ever Make Love To a Tree?

The Golden Bush is not the Burning Bush. No Biblical mumbo jumbo here. The Golden Bush stands sturdy, upright, catching all the sun's rays in leafy hair. The wind caresses his worried brow. Rubbing up against his skin gives me the voice to bark. I want to linger in the shade of beauty, hold close to his amber light.

Behold all nature. Don't control it. Love. Stamina to stay firmly planted on this earth. Move in those earth bound rhythms. No matter how cold the wind blows. Above it all, protected by some incandescent umbrella, stands the mighty Golden Bush.

Now, as legend of the Golden Bush goes, when gods of old saw the mother goddess caressing the Golden Bush; they became jealous. They sent thunder, lightning, great floods, pestilence. The mother goddess sent her spirit, an eternal nymph, with a Golden Apple from the Golden Bush. The nymph gave the apple to Zeus, Thor and Jupiter. After they ate of it's flesh, a great peaceful love came over them. They withdrew their chaos. They sent those known as the watchers down to protect the bush and his earthly lover.

These watchers descended into Druids, Shamans and keepers of the flame. Some mystics say that this is the true story of the Garden Of Eden.

The gods asked in return, that the mother goddess only visit the bush when there was fruit to bear She must also never reveal the secret of her endless love to mortals. To this day, the woman who gives freely of her body and her spirit to a Merlin of the wood risks her very soul.
Yet, all life rejoices when she does.

Evergreen as though it be. The cradle will rock. Then spring becomes the summer. As above, so below.

the golden fruit.

hangs just so.

Unlike Newton's, it never falls.

Burning Down The Baby Factory

Deep into my fourth and last pregnancy, early in the year '72, I sat on my front porch swing and plotted to become a Catholic outlaw.

 at least...that's what the priest said I would end up as
 at least..that's what my then husband expounded on
 at least...that's what all my rigid, religious friends thought

Now, burning down the baby factory was inevitable. Much like the strategic plans made by the rebels during a military take over. Months later, waddling over the 290 expressway bridge with my new baby boy in hand. I stopped and wondered why, anyone would make an expressway under such a devoted ritual pathway to and from the holy temple. They passed there those pilgrims on their way to the weekly Sunday ritual. I stared down at the population of cars, trucks and moving metal. It occurred to me, at that moment, that this place reeked of sacrificial images. Much like the pagan places in the world where such pathways to the alter of the Aztec sun god or the Hindu Black Kali are marked with unmistakable sounds and smells.

How easy, I thought it would be for some modern day scapegoat or self-appointed lamb to climb the frail rail fence and tumble forward onto the vehicle parade below.

The god of band-aids came into my life that day. He touched me through the deft craft of one Japanese wonder surgeon located on Michigan avenue.

For a high priced fee, the Japanese wonder would invoke the band-aid god to come forth for any woman. Any woman willing to pay the price.

It was a rather painless process. The stay in the hospital was merely overnight. The band-aids came off in a week. My then partner either feeling betrayed or trying to save me from hell or both, yelled at me as I was being wheeled down the hall,

" You'll Be Excommunicated ! "

After the quick laser prick, he stated that I had actually taken away his manhood.

Much, much later, I told him that I would rather be the pilot of my own plane, than fly stand-by on his heaven over hell, helicopter mentality.

Having no fear of flying or of hitting the pavement, that night I had a Hot Lips Houlihan kind of dream. Echoes of frantic, yet comic M.A.S.H type messages and music still invade my mind whenever I walk over that bridge.

" Chopper One   Chopper One
   going down   going down

    heading into a metal parade
    seems like a natural disaster

     Medical Emergenc
     Medical Emergency

For god's sake bring more than band-aids "

A Bottle of Red
Halloween, Old Town 1981

    DBL has it now sitting next to some other Haitian art somewhere on the near south side, not far from where the Elvis Shrine appeared. Red jewels cover, encrusted from lip to the body. Toil of an expert hand-held Haitian. Blood red with pearls and tiny stones, shells, grit, peices of 'ate. Shipped with art from that hallowed isle when all of Oak Street scrambled to seek you out, own your heart, keep those apart, break a new start.
    He took you graciuosly, my prize. My well-worn costume prize for a kalidscope Shiva .
    "Shake any dead men from their graves lately ?
    Take the bottle, not the money " he whispered.
    Inside loomed great rocks of brown crystal, jewels of naked consciousness, known archives, never-before dreams. Raising the jewled lady figure to our lips, still invoking the spirit of Samhain we drank our own shadow wine.
    We stopped monmentarily to spy the Hotel Lincoln's neon. As always, it was malfunctioning. We toasted all the writers who may have stayed there then sped back to the hidden coach house on Wells street in the V-8 Olds with terminal deacy.
    Shortly after this Herod's night, the good news came.
    " Your dying... but we want to try a new proceedure, a transplant. Best surgeon in the country".
    Prinz was an expert. He agreed also not to use my legs but put the vital thing in my arm instead. I watched my operation from from another realm and the team was splendid. Finally, they did bring me round with only a slightly loosened front tooth.
    The confines of the red bottle flow through all our veins.
    So, sip as sweet as shadow wine.

The Secret Heart Of A Flame

" Who are you "
throaty caterpillar voice booms

*Paraphrased
by Del Close*

Ran into a foolish moth the other day.
He was tryin' to batter his way into a
200 watt light bulb with his head
" Moth... I said ...What is it with you.
Are you suicidal or what. Don't you know
you're courtin' death by bashing your
brains out with your head. "
He turned and looked at me with those
honey combed eyes of his and said,
" Haven't you ever seen the secret heart of
a flame. We rare breed of moths would rather
wad our lives into a ball and toss it all into
the fire than live one day bogged down
in the mire ". With that the little blighter
flew into the business end of a zippo
windproof lighter. Poof ! No more little blighter.
That moth may have been crazy but I wish I
wanted something as much as he wanted
to fry.

    I met John the night he died. I met Del the director of Second City shortly after that. I was looking for my boots left at a former workshop with Sills, the original Second City guru, instigator of improvisation.
    Like a cat and a mouse, me under the table, rump in the air. The air heavy with last night's smoke and performance.
    " Who Are You" the throaty caterpillar voice booms
    " Who are you , glass Alice refrains,
       I'm looking for my boots ".

" Well come back when you find them "

    I did. It was John who told me to find Del. Del, the director of Second City for 17 years. Second City doorway to a billion journeys to the beyond. Equally a training camp and front line *blow your mind while you still have it* kind of place. An ongoing saga of modern theatrical display rising out of the University of Chicago's gut. Spewing kernels of truth portraying human archtypes in the news, and in the moment happenings. Second City, Chi town personified. Grandmother to Saturday Night Live. Stomping ground of those wishing something wonderful right away.

    Bibliographers and writers paint Del as a pathological hippy, Bernie kept him on as director even though the feds came swooping down all over Old Town for years after Belushi popped. Bernie knew no one could, no one has yet directed a better show, that got better reviews, made more money, made more stars than Del did. He was founder of countless improvizarios, instigator of many into the drug culture, and listed as house metaphysician on early Saturday Night Live Shows, before John died.

    Del taught me things he didn't know he was teaching me. Me, dying of some obscure bone disease that doctors kept giving me Valium for.

~~Dr.~~ actual   Can't find problem... give Valium
~~note~~   keep patient from freaking

    My bones cracking from some hidden magnetizing force, were 80% dissolved by the time I was properly diagnosed.
    It was John who said
    " Leap to the edge if you seek you "

It was John waving going out as I was coming in that fate filled night. Two souls on the same cosmic road. He spoke to me right before his silver cord broke.

" Way to go... Use it to go back.
　Use it to go the other way.
　I've always used it to get out.

Say Hi to Del when you find him."

With that I felt left behind. Witness to an historical event. Awed by his friendliness. On his last trip and he knew it. He knew one day it would happen. The coke fairy would one day collect her real fee. He was ready not to return.
　　　I remember his face. He was happy and sad. Sad that people would not understand and happy that he was making the final trip. He sashayed his way around the others rolling the final steps to the beyond. He cut in front of them
　　　　patted their behinds
　　　　twirled on one foot
　　　　making them laugh.

Crazy and sane at the same time.

The Unicorn Connection

Done as a performance peice

Have you ever felt like an Armadillo
has life ever made you hide in a shell
then carry it around with you
just in case life becomes hell

        I dreamt was a Unicorn
        lovely and free
        there aren't many of us
        we were sacrificed to the sea

Some knights saved us from dragons
what a glorious sight
only to bring us to servitude
night after glorious knight

        We were the first extinct species
        both a rare and magical find
        we had a grand genteel beauty
        we still have a unique sort of a mind

You did not know women once were Unicorns ?
that just goes to show
what men have forgotten
what some women know

        You long for our comfort
        chase our behinds
        you capture to save us

In there lies the charm

You threaten to leave us to fate
so we follow our fellow
till love turns to hate
then you chide us for being
just something you ain't

That's when I awoke crying

> *Wherefore art thou Lancelot*
> *Wherefore art thou....*

        The it all began one sunny day
        this friend of mine came out to play
        after months of being friend
        he kissed me like other men had done

He had this part
it was his heart
it made me see how fragile and beautiful
he really was

I had grown to trust him

        I trust you so I said
        then he led me
        to the bed ... it was a couch really
        then the floor
        on it went
        more and more

In due time I did question this configuration

He pulled away
I let him go
just long enough before I shook the pole
to see if the big fish was still there

This was the best of id
we played each other
yes we did
playing notes without a care
phantom in your opera chair

I'm abreast the throne
I'd say
off we rode into the night of the longest day

                        Mid-summer's night
                        it was right for me
                        to hold him
                        lifted up to mania heights
                        this goddess shown
                        it was right for me to hold him
                        my moonbeams striking every
                        corner every soft fold
                        hugging every hairy place
                        when I turned and looked back
                        in his face he saw
                        the cosmic principle of light
                        I brought it back into him

Our eyes were open to the soul
what poured out upon the whole world
was love and light
we really glowed
friends told us so

                        me my heart became so strong
                        and free something I thought
                        was never possible for me
                        at least upon this earth
                        by his clumsiness

        He gave me birth

No It was not painful
like the first time
>
> This new born chick
> just lapped it up
> got so involved in
> bottom's up
> I wanted just
> to eat him up
> so I did

Then he sat me down one day and said
I think you love me
more than I love you
makes me feel
guilty and bemused
don't know what I want
I'm so confused
>
> So my moonman
> my panda
> my pooh
> he went back to being
> who knows who

Here I stand again
a unicorn among men
If I could lose my horn
I might fit in
be someone's perfect woman
When I do try with all my might
what's wrong is still wrong
That which is wrong is somehow so very right
I know there are no shining white knights
I know moonbeams glisten
on starry starry nights
Yet in my dreams I cry most every night

Wherefore art thou my Lancelot
Wherefore art thou..

Woman of Wonder

Woman On The Edge

Woman on the edge is like a cat
on a ledge
she fluidly moves forward

Woman on the edge of her seat
during afternoon heat
moves toward
the tip
of her own iceberg
floating below
stands seeking
eyes sweeping
moving back
tunneled
through time
falling
slipping
to the edge of her mind

Woman on the edge
of a bed
stretches
one leg
up
over his head
lips full
hips pull
while fan overhead
hums
spins
the sweet fragrance

A *New Kind of* Baby

baby   baby   baby
" Oh, sweet baby "

Please daddy....

    Let me hear those words whispered soft against my ear. A daddy's a word. It's clearly a word just stuck in my throat. Not known here within. But he's there in that lost everywhile. I'm there locked in his smile.

    Being a daddy has nothing to do with being a father. A father is the Heirophant. But a daddy, a daddy is the universe.

    Having found the puzzle pieces, fit them to this frame. Lost no longer in my ego, I need not to understand. It goes deeper than any feeling. It survives the common man.

> Is this water for the drinking
> Is this lovely outstretched hand
> one of friendship
> or betrayal

    Only time can watch a baby. Catch a daddy if you can. S-strip him down to barest sweetness. S-s-teal and peal away his hard ass stand.

Until my daddy hears me.
Wraps baby in his arms.
I'll just be a waiting Mustang. You know the kind,
Loaded, four on the floor, built for speed.

    Tread not on sacred water
    Tip-toe not on sacred bones

  Be the sacred daughter with spirit forged
from holy ground. Forsake no magic in the process.
Protection is the worst.
It keeps one from becoming.
Keeps me cloaked and waiting.
    Not my chosen game.

    Come to me
    sweet note daddy
    as I breathe your love
    it sings

    You are that breathless
    holding motion
    come be the wind
    beneath my wings

Then maybe
someday,
I'll get to be a new kind of baby.

Eyes Of The Dragon

You are the eyes of the dragon
for you rock my very soul
lost forever in your flower garden
I am lost forever in your smile

    Men I've known can't shake me
    yet you rock my very soul

    Vision quest you eyes
    so they can see mine
    pierce my heart
    you cannot hurt
    dragon lift
    scale
    higher
    past the stairwells of divine

    Deep with in the darkness of your plaza
    in the doll house of your mind
    lays the iron
    you must forge it
    breathe your fire
    roast me well

You are the eyes of the dragon
rock and roll my very soul
sweet dragon eyes of thunder
rock my hips till I roll under
lost forever in your smile

Too Easy

If you want to let them kill you, go ahead. Don't think that they wouldn't if they could. Kill you and get away with I mean. Why ? There is no why when there's an eye locked, heart rocked, bone knocked notion.

Listen up babe ! You gave it to them. Sure they knew you would give it to someone so why not them

why not

You could have listened to your friends. The ones that knew what was really going on/ All men know these things. You are all descended from some ancient race of bloodhound.

Here boy....

Hither he comes. Low thou doest thou really need to use your nose. Aren't your eyes and bassett ears enough for you to drink it in, and by the way, your red hair's getting thin. Your muscle heart does beat. The others not so tough. The last memory I have of you is picking shit on Paulina street. Your nose moist. Your eyes pink. Just running with the hounds. Made me think... what a man for all seasons you think you are.
Listen up ol' pup. Sniff your brain some reason. Fantasy flights are all you have left. You hound for any season.

go on... shoo

Catch up with those on the scent of their next kill. You will find one. Hopefully she'll get away slightly wounded. But you, you're destined to remain wrapped in your barbed wire.

Wondering why you're not a lair
just an asshole
sniffing out the scent of man's decent
into the womb
that rejects him

That will become your final hell

When you catch the little fox
you hound
yell

But remember
the goddess
will be watching

        Does anyone know what
        a man for all seasons is

        Is he worth his salt
        Or does he only pepper
        you with his words

        If he makes an honest woman
        of you
        what the hell does that make him

Red Hot Mama

Red hot candle light by wonderlake burned that summer where youthful knight with lady fair rode time again on his mechanical steed. The Harley hum would awaken her to put on those aqua pocket Palmento jeans. The moon smilin' down all the while as if approvin' of this *Tess of D' urbervilles* disappearance.
The heat/moon/strength of his backside all blurred into motion with his soft shadow pressin' into hers.
Red Hot Mama flickered.

Morning breezes blow mock memories of that other life. That other time. A time when adaptability eventually buried. Time relentless as the tide washing away, building character along the craggy shore. Thoughts turn to that lost life. The need to debauch the wife. The chaotic family strife steeped in daughters pain. Pain harbored in a heart. It strikes out like lashing winds transformed through time. Again to be the slap. The slap she just refused to stand there and take. Take with grace. The good woman gone bad... or mad syndrome. A woman in love who had had enough. Enough to light a candle at both ends. So, red hot mama flickered.

Adaptability preserves the species. She found those jeans the other day, put them on. Alone and simply single, she gazed amazed the way they fit her even better now. Her eyes pierced the glass between the years. She almost felt his hands hot. Lingerin' Ghosts of lust lost whispered,
" Red hot mama can't you image such machinery aglow again".
Her spirit not withstanding sins and shame, she wears it ever so softly on her brow.

A Woman In Love

A woman in love is so damn insecure
We say that we're not
But the message
is clear
Men invoke us to love them
somehow we do
then little by little
a check point
we do
When I'm with you
I am certain
but when you're away
my longing to touch you gets
in the way
So what is it
I wonder
when distance and time
makes my heart stutter
is it you
or this longing
that makes me like butter
If I could reach out
right now with this hand
my soul would touch yours
as we laugh/stand
shining/peaceful
in each other's light
loving you
loving me
makes everything right
But a woman in love
is such an insecure thing
Call me
call me
make that telephone ring

Rhinos In The Moonlight

There's a map
upon your body
        (can't you see it)
look
most any night
it directs the outward flow of traffic
it is a boundary to the right
to the left lies lighted limbo
        You, oh poet
        who expresses life
        infect your vision with the moon

Be spontaneous
oh poet
if thy be at all
personify thy notion
check out its' anatomy
treat the night as a Madonna
go beyond

Be a rhino in the moonlight

Trip past thy own creative feet
wear your armor as amour
trade it in for 3-d glasses

The middle of the moment is
where all psychic surgery begins

Bare the message of the moment
be the door through which
all may pass
though you may not

Ticket To Ride

    Stop
    Start
    Put me on Hold

    Just give me my ticket to ride

Is this the right day, time, place.
Probably not. Never is. Never will be.
Is this the final hour.

    Just give me my ticket to ride

Go sell your dreams to someone on the right.
I'm movin' on down this road, layin' a strip.
Burnin' more than your precious rubber could
ever take. When I take my ticket, I'm not takin'
the pain of the world with me.

Now on hold, I take that pain in my hands.
Let it wash through me. In my deepest sleep
        catch it
        change it
        poke it
        kiss it
        make it
        change it till it filters out

Till it becomes something else.
Sometimes something wonderful.

Transformation is not an occupation.

Believe it or not
what you see
is not what you get

Just give me my ticket to ride.

Stop
Start
Put me on hold

Is this the final hour ?
Is love ever unconditional ?
Is unrequited love really
a dying swan or merely a goose ?
Does anybody ever answer these
damned questions ?

Haven't you ever felt the terror within
Hasn't it ever tried to grip you firmly ?

If you feel to the nines
as much as you are up
you fall to that darkness
eagerly awaiting your plunge

I don't try to block it
play the idea out
as much as I possibly can

In playing with my mind
my heart becomes the devil's advocate
It becomes an intellectual game
Mind blocks the ride stops
clearly as a goal spread upon the ice

Just give me my ticket to ride.

I'll rev those engines back up.
Begin my next climb.
It will become a spin
then the ultimate dive.
Guess I'm just enthralled
by the motion of it all.

If the dive ever becomes
too strong
too full
to ever pull out of
it will be because of this form
a rose
only open, never bud like
in my blooming
finds this outer crust
too horrible to remain imprisoned within
any longer

Then my spirit can
no longer deny
that one final lover
who will hold me closer
     tighter
     longer
Than any human lover
I have ever known.
The spirit of Merlin must be free.
  Just give me my ticket...

When I finally take that ride,
I'll be able to speak without talking
be the laugh you hear through the wind
be but a smile upon your lips and in your dreams...
   and in your dreams.

The

Miami Series

Nite Not Alone

He stares me down.

The sweetest eyes, I've ever seen, in a room that dust forgot, in a place, soft focus frame.

Light streaming from those eyes, the sweetest, I ever saw, bounces 'cross the room from mirror to mirror to memories...a thousand message years into the future.

This sealed like tomb heavy with ritual, like a darkened zoom lens capturing some historic sight. If it were there. Some cosmic creature above me whispers love songs while I toss in my sleep. Perched upon the pillow next to my head lies Carl, C.G. *daddio* Jung.
He looks and over looks this whole slumbering scene in silence from the cover of his best selling book, *A Myth In Our Time.* "Good Company she keeps, even when she sleeps," the voice declares.

Madshine begins to twinkle in those eyes as the vision starts to move within. The water bed bearing down, sucking him in. Terror itching at the corner of his mind. He leaps up.
Darts around this ridiculously, rituallly rigged room, a full circle of light. Probably wondering how the hell he got in here, in the first place, desperately trying to depart.
Hmmm. The thought of it, I thought. Hmmm. Well, whomever he is, he must belong here. I wondered what else he knew. I wondered if he knew sex was better on the living room floor.

>   Unchanged, he stares me down.

Then the vision starts to fade.
The silence crests to a wave.
Carl, C.G. *daddio,* Jung bid him come here.
See me.
Watch me.
Watch me dream him.

The vision fades
as I slip softly into tomorrow in his arms.
The sleeper most sound, I smile.

>   End of vision.

>   **End of Nite Not Alone.**

I Want To Run

I want to run and live naked on a key

Be thee one with the sand, sea, birds

Pelican my mind again
dive down through peacock colored waves
to fish me out
hold me tenderly in your mouth

Make no mistake
the wave is always there
phantom's deep inside your soul

Break away from silly notions
hard line movements
time clocks
machines

End your mindless obsession with money
it has been known to make men
commit war
murder their wives
steal cars

Take my hand with the sea standing witness
play crab in the sacred stones
slip into the white surf

Greet the Great Eastern Sun
with the landscape of your life
held tightly in your hand
& in my heart

Ode To...

Chicago Buds and floods spring forth

The city's bowels
are filled with abundant fluids

I've never seen you quite this way
city, Lady On The Make

    Oh, I've seen you, screened you, imbibed you.
I've seen you laughing, stretching in the sun.
I've seen you dirty, beggin' to be washed. I've seen
you gently sigh, while lover Lake Mich kisses your
toes. You like it.
    Yet, you still long for that Ocean Lover denied
you due to your proximity. If you could pick up and
move your cement skirts and sky scraper hats to stick
your tired eyes and sandstones into the sea.
You would.

You'd make history again.
You'd make headlines again.

HEADLINE

NATURAL PHENOMENON STRIKES MID-WEST
The City Of Chicago
Has Just Got Up and Moved
After spending the night in the
Blue Ridge Mountains
She is making a direct march on Miami Shores.

Maybe then hard-edged lady of:

> hog butchers
> improvised theater
> atom bomb births
> & Democratic conventions

Maybe then your heart can beat in rhythm with nature not progress.

Maybe then your heart can
beat
in rhythm
with nature not progress

You lose nothing but your prostitution to the mid-west mentality.

> Men may miss you
> > curse you
> > blame you
> > try to recreate you

Yet, you know the kiss
of he who beholds only beauty and light
he loves you
You
& you finally know it
at long last

Unbridled

4 am
the sun is not up yet
I am

It's not birds chirping mad beaks off
It's not the red sky muddy with rain

It is
the sound of the crowd
as we near the finish line
two turf runners
on the race track of the world
bred of sturdy hoof
tireless of spirit
like steeple chasers from Connamara
connected way past legend
back to a primitive time
the crude Irish drum and flute
playing the strains of clan
Red O'Neil
while we turn turf
bump butts on the back stretch
hustle our way through the pack
neck n' neck
we're out in front
hindquarter to hindquarter

nostrils flaring
hoofbeats and hearts daring
racin' gainst the wind
countdown to the wire
rain only eggs us on
turfrunners make good mudders
even beyond the loving cup
they love the cool sod under their
beaten hoofs
race our hearts
our minds
break all records
to the winner's circle of the soul
more than history
we will become legend
once again

The 60's Ain't Over Yet

Inhale
flavor breathes the air
toasted almonds toast
fan dancers

Beware
beside the blueberry muffins
lurks a sign
that screams
No Exit

There's
a harvest of dream weavers
youth mist
tourists

" Come on give us your best shot "

all seem to say
with their outward stance
reflection children
of the American Dream

But in the 60's
peace
was the motive
and the movement

In the 60's
no training camps for 90's drop outs

In the 60's
no establishment entrepreneurs
capitalizing on being 60's

In the 60's
no children of 90's drop outs
maquerading in their parents' garb

The beats were different
they spoke out
speaking
political/philosophical flowers
of the truth of
Armageddon
while the rest of the world
dallied in the suburbs of their minds
watching the 6 o'clock news
report casualties of our youth
fighting
a prime time war

There is an exit

It is the door to one's own enlightenment

Some may be that door
some may never know
the difference

Meeting Allen

    The door is open before we get there. He occupies the favorite northwest corner apartment each summer. He is departing for New York once again. Stepping out onto the balcony one can see the beloved flat irons. After a warm welcome, he and my friend chat. He is most amiable.

    A man with a video camera buzzing around shooting and talking, interrupts. Demanded to speak, he wiggles free, Eventually he speaks on camera, profoundly tells of gathering rose buds while you may, bridging the gap of all who are present. It's a bit of a dance. Others come in. One begs for an autograph then giggles as she almost smears the ink. My friend tries to help him tie up a box bound for New York. The dance continues.

    " Got your Camera, Allen",
    a voice across the room asks.

    Sitting in his masterful white leather chair, without being asked, I watch the revolving scene. We talk as if we are old friends. Another picture taker... another fan... another student comes in to say good-by. He remains gracious while others dance in and out. He finishes tasks like a last minute dab of refrigerator cleaning. He cares how he leaves things. I ask if he would like help. He responds with,
    " Why are you a feminist ? "
    We both laugh

C.D. Talk
Book Talk
Other Talk

Finally, the dance comes to an end. He offers his card to one of the camera people.

" May I have one ", I ask

" Oh, this is my last one "

" May I Have it ". I stretch out my hand.

He smiles and hands it to me. Hugs and kisses wholeheartedly bestowed upon my friend, as dearly as the moment we walked in. I take his hand and say,
" It's been a real pleasure."

He looks at my friend knowingly as if we are in love. That's why I am there. He wanted me to meet Allen.

In the parking lot my friend says,

" He really likes you.

You were great ! "

This Is The House

This is the house of broken dreams
      of a place called mine
    of family
where dreams lay silent
waiting for their moment
slowly disappearing

It was here my heart was happy
if not for long

It was here my children born began their
own dreams, dreams that have come true,
dreams still growing

It was here my mother finally had a house
if only while on visits.

It was here my oldest married
set a time for me to ponder

It was here my heart healed
while my body dodged the death dance

It was here my vision met me
smack upon a winter's dawn
soft as snow flakes never melting
in the hold/cold hand

This is the house of broken dreams
where the lady before me died in her bedroom

After hearing
I changed bedrooms

Silent in her grave
Does she know my life and her death are part of
the same sentence

That we looked through the same windows
cooked on the same stove
smiled on the front porch swing
smelled the same roses

This is the house
of family split
of brawls no more
of dreams anew

This is the house
where visions sprang
from mirrors to real life
where memory dreams
become the life you seize
for it is there

This is the house
of faulty starts
of new beginnings

Where I read/wrote/wondered
where I could breathe
where I shut the world out
where I slowly began to open my heart
began to dream a new dream

Once I started dreaming there was no end to it
the dreams came true
they are still forming

As I leave this house
of memories behind me
(caution tossed with things away)

I keep close to me the person who became me

Poet

evermore

Amid Crashing Iron

Turning gears on the wheel of progress
Be it New York, Miami, L.A. We loved
We pondered our art
our true lives purpose

Journeying on crowed X ways filled
with endless construction
Waiting for sewer trains to speed us out on
sub-subterranean rails
high above the cities' squalor

Drinking life in

Visiting favorite book stores
                 we eat and drink word images
                like vocabulary vampires

Sucking in as many as we need to feel full

Sipping strong coffee
     saki
                 we are like wine soaked berries

Burying memories of crashing iron
               bridges breaking
               scaping towards skyhood

Painting us into each others canvas
               we begin to hear music of
               new rhythms as poets do

Straining to the silent be-bop symphony
               which beckons us to beat each
               others' tambourine, let

Crashing iron clank out a distant note

on sea soaked sand
                        I shake my feather

If The Key Fits

Spa Lady

I tread the boardwalk on rollerskates. My mind returns to the sea. The sea brought me here. Brought me to be the goddess of the beaches bound up in leather and wheels. My mind speaks. The ocean hums. The sea has always had this conversation with me whenever I stand before it, silly in sand, a song in my heart.

Now, down in the tropics everything's different. Fat white cats from Chicago sit with lizards in the linen closet sharing hidden bliss. Neither knows the other's there. Down here everything's different. Water smells different. Water is color. Water is land. Water is boiled by mid-western woman with sensitive systems. Roaches like small mice claim their right to be called palm bugs.

I finish this in shadows of early morning soft key breezes, 100 feet from light blue waters of the gulf. New Year's morn on a Key-side resort with a whole paradise at my feet. Missing Chicago, I see her rise up. Dangling from Neptune's belt as if strung on a chain, flung far from the Florida finger, pointing the way to new doors. A mystery of crystal She.

He trusts you easier than I, Spa Lady, green and gloriously weedy. He is a Florida Boy born to nature.

Keys Of Coral Reef

If you play the Torch key
high or low

If you Pine it Big
or Largo long enough

You find the green stuff
bunched in Saddles
numbered like horses
1-2-3

If you think you know
their names
guess again
Sugarloaf just slices into many

The door of tropic perception
beckons each car to
slip the ribbon road

west

KeyWest

    Tee tops

    Sun shops

    Glasses

                      Crop boys

                      Pottery

                      Coy glances

Tourists wander
dazed

Car waits by gay boy shop

A quarter buys more time
A dollar buys more
A dollar per tourist per square foot

Key West for sale

Key West For Sale

Up the street with trash and cobblestones
lies a tiny house
inside no one abides
but termites and memories
so putrid it makes the floor slant
the bed beg to be taken out into the sun
and burnt

    " Ninety thousand " quips
      a too serious Realtor

I think of bursting into laughter
run out the door
into the tropic air
to look for you

You who have already bolted
from the confines of this ugly little shack
that limps along
begging
for someone
with a big ax to put it out of it's misery

Hometown Son

Hometown son
Follow the Great Eastern sun
Never look back

Unable to plunge past
some unthinkable hour

Stop the dance

Let them spin

Hometown son
They thought they knew you

Tell bulls/bells
Keep moving
Never stop

Words become
more than friends
Blazing a way
to step into

To step

beyond

Paradise

When Ernie came here it was.

Gem of tropical punch
perpetrated by tourist paychecks
surrounded by constant fishing boats

you bid all come

stay

You wily them with baited palms
You waken them with dreams of splendor

You may or may not speak the truth
It doesn't matter

Paradise is paradise in the garden
of the sea

In the secret garden

of your soul

About the author

Rose Virgo, a native of Chicago's South side, is considered one of the top performance poets in the poetry scene today. She developed her performance style on Chicago's varied range of audiences: beatnik-style, slam, performance poetry, concert poetry, and poetry video. She draws her performance techniques from drama, improvisation and a rhythmic blend from her years as dancer/choreographer.

Rose was the named 1991 Hemingway poet by the Hemingway Foundation, Oak Park, Illinois. She founded Artists Against Violence. She also founded Artists Against Violence Towards Women, Poetry In The Park and hosted The Wednesday Nite Poetry Series at the Above Ground Coffee House in Oak Park.

Rose is also a member of The Beyond Poets, a music-performance poetry ensemble. The Beyond Poets tour the U.S. during the summer months.

Rose is the mother of four children, and a graduate of Northeastern Illinois University.